Tracking Through Argument

KINGSCOURT / McGRAW-HILL

Tracking Through Argument
Copyright © 2001 Rigby Heinemann

Rigby is part of Harcourt Education, a division of
Reed International Books Australia Pty Ltd ABN 70 001 002 357.

Edited by Simone Calderwood
Text by Black Dog Books
Teaching notes by Maureen Hyland and Martin Dean
Designed by Jennifer Johnston
Photographic research by Janet Pheasant

Acknowledgments
for photographs: © Auscape/Francois Gohier, pp. 6 (foreground), 9;
© Auscape/Jean-Marc La Roque, p. 10 (bottom right); © Auscape/T.
Shivanandappa, p. 16; © Australian Picture Library, p. 17; © Australian
Picture Library/Alex Bartel, p. 26 (bottom); © Australian Picture Library/
Esther Beaton, p. 27 (middle); © Australian Picture Library/Gary Bell,
p. 11; © Australian Picture Library/John Carnemolla, pp. 10 (bottom
left), 12; © Australian Picture Library/Greenpeace/Morgan, pp. 6
(background), 7; © Australian Picture Library/Nick Rains, p. 27 (top);
© Australian Picture Library/Zefa, p. 10 (top right); Malcolm Cross,
cover, title page, pp. 26 (top), 28, 29 (bottom); all other images
PhotoDisc.
for illustrations: Ian Forss, pp. 4, 22, 23.

KINGSCOURT/McGRAW-HILL

Shoppenhangers Road, Maidenhead
Berkshire, SL6 2QL
Telephone: 01628 502730

Fax: 01628 635895

www.kingscourt.co.uk
E-mail: enquiries@kingscourt.co.uk

Printed in Australia by Advance Press

10 9 8 7 6 5 4 3 2 1

ISBN: 0-07-710330-0

Contents

Introduction to
Persuasive Texts

WE PROMISE this book will help you to understand the art of persuasion!

Did you notice that a promise has just been made to you? You were offered the chance to find out something. We tried to get you interested.

When you try to persuade people, you need to get them interested. You need to offer or give the reader something. That could mean giving them information or facts. You could offer to do something for them in return for a favour. For instance you could say, "Mum, can I stay up and watch TV all night? I'll do the washing up for the rest of the month." Or "If you give me some of your lollies, I'll always give you some of mine."

As long as what you ask for is reasonable and what you offer is believable, then you have a good chance of getting what you want.

In this book, there are news reports, letters to the editor, advertisements, community letters and posters all designed to be persuasive. Many different tricks are used to persuade people. As you read, you can decide for yourself whether these tricks work.

In presenting a persuasive text, the author aims to convince the reader that something is true. Such a text might attempt to make you believe that a certain product is the best, that a particular decision is right, that an attitude is the correct one to have, or that a certain viewpoint is the only option in a situation.

The author will strongly reinforce his or her point of view with supportive facts or information, but will not present an alternative to an argument or a possible option when a problem needs to be solved.

The language used in the text will often be directed at the reader's emotions. The author will use words that make the reader feel sympathetic, annoyed, encouraged or opposed to a situation with the aim of making the reader agree with his or her point of view.

Evidence or information from famous people or experts will often be used to reinforce and support the view being presented.

If we are aware of the tactics used in presenting a persuasive text, then we will be in a better position to form our own opinions and develop our own ideas.

Forms of Persuasive Texts:
News articles, documentaries, editorial opinions, advertisements, complaints, persuasive essays

Purpose:
To explain and analyse events, phenomena or issues by putting forward an argument or point of view. The author states and justifies his or her point of view.

Structure:
- Introduce the topic.
- Present a point of view.
- Elaborate on the topic by providing background information that supports the point of view.
- Each argument that is put forward is supported by evidence, for example, statistics or quotes from experts.
- Reiterate the point of view and emphasise the general issues. Can also include ideas for action from the reader.

Gentle Whales, Deadly Harpoons

By our special contributor, Doris Fishy of the Green Dreaming Environmental Lobby Group

WHALES are the world's largest mammals. Yet these gentle giants that roam our oceans are no match for the deadly harpoons on Japanese whaling ships. While the rest of the world looks on, the Japanese have continued to slaughter whales to be sold as meat in the Japanese markets. They claim the killing is for scientific purposes only.

Now the Japanese are adding two endangered species, Bryde's and Sperm whales, to their hunting list. Neither of these whales has been hunted since commercial whaling was banned in 1986.

It is time to do more than just ask for a halt to these vicious murders. Japan must be convinced that the rest of the world will not sit still and do nothing.

This Sperm whale is an endangered species.

The best way to get Japan's attention is to apply trade bans. As soon as people cannot sell their goods, or buy the things that they want, they will realise that whaling is an issue the world takes seriously.

Fishery experts say that if hunting is not stopped now, some species will no longer be endangered. **They will be extinct.**

There are claims that whale meat is a part of the traditional Japanese diet. But the traditional method of catching whales in nets from small boats has been replaced with modern industrial methods of killing from large ships. Since modern methods of killing were introduced more than one hundred years ago, the numbers of whales killed has meant that, every year, more species are becoming endangered.

Fishery experts say that if hunting is not stopped now, some species will no longer be endangered. They will be extinct.

The Sperm whale can grow as long as twenty metres and weigh up to sixty tonnes. That's a lot of meat for the Japanese markets and a big profit for the whale killers. Profit, not tradition, is the driving force behind the continued slaughter of these helpless creatures.

A Japanese whaling ship preparing to load a harpooned whale.

The United States is considering introducing trade penalties against Japan, and the governments of Australia, New Zealand and Britain have backed the move. We call on the governments to do more now. Stop imports of Japanese goods until Japan stops killing whales.

Write to your politicians. Save the whales.

Exploring Persuasive Texts— Gentle Whales, Deadly Harpoons

In the previous article "Gentle Whales, Deadly Harpoons", the author relies heavily upon emotive language to convince the reader that what the Japanese people are doing to the whales is very wrong. The author uses words such as "gentle" and "helpless" when describing the whales. This is in contrast to the words such as "deadly", "slaughter", "killing" and "vicious murders" to describe the actions of the Japanese. The writer's intention is that the reader will immediately begin to sympathise with the whales.

Let's explore this persuasive writing in more detail. Look at some of the following sentences from "Gentle Whales, Deadly Harpoons".

> "Yet these **gentle** giants that roam our oceans are no match for the **deadly** harpoons on Japanese whaling ships."

The writer is implying that the whales are innocent and they are being pursued by the might of the deadly harpoons. Note the use of the emotive adjectives "deadly" and "gentle".

> "…the Japanese have continued to **slaughter** whales to be **sold as meat** in the Japanese markets. They claim the **killing** is for scientific purposes only."

The writer is questioning the Japanese claim that the killing is for scientific purposes, and is strongly implying these claims are false. This is supported by the assertion that the whale meat is sold at food markets.

▶ **"**Fishery **experts** say that if hunting is not stopped now, some species will no longer be endangered. *They will be extinct*.**"**

In this sentence, the writer presents information supplied by experts to support her point of view. In the short sentence, note the use of strong language and the future tense.

▶ **"Profit**, not tradition, is the driving force behind the continued slaughter of these **helpless** creatures.**"**

Financial benefit is strongly stated as the reason behind the killing of the whales, yet the writer provides no evidence to support this statement.

▶ **"We** call on the governments to do more now. *Stop* imports of Japanese goods until Japan *stops* killing whales.**"**

Now that the writer feels that she has strongly presented her point of view and convinced her readers, she includes the readers (through the use of the word "we") in her call for action against Japan.

▶ **"**Write to your politicians. *Save* the whales.**"**

The article ends with a personal plea to involve the reader and a request that the reader takes action. Again, note the short sentences that give a strong impression of urgency.

What Have **you** Done Today to Save Our Planet?

The planet is dying.

**Our climate is warming up.
Our oceans are rising.
Our air is polluted.**

Join an environmental group today.
Good intentions are not enough!

**Act now.
Before it is too late!**

Tracking Through Argument

Our oceans' biggest **killer** is not the shark.

It's the plastic bag!

Exploring **Persuasive** Texts
—Magazine Advertisements

In the environmental posters on pages 10 and 11, emotive images are used to reinforce the text. In fact, the images of environmental pollution are more powerful than the text.

Certain words are emphasised in the design to attract the reader's attention. The powerful text is in the present tense. The writer appeals directly to the reader to take action. This ensures that the problem presented becomes a personal issue and not just one that can be left for others to solve.

Powerful images are used to highlight what is happening to the air around us. The chimney is seen to dwarf the surrounding towns, creating the impression of a dominating force.

The photographs of oil-covered and dead animals present a sense of helplessness. These creatures are innocent victims of humans' inappropriate actions.

> **"What Have _YOU_ Done Today to Save Our Planet?"**

The reader is addressed with a question. What action have you, the reader, taken to save the planet? The reader is asked to question his or her involvement. Focus is also placed on the word "you". The writer may have the intention of making the reader feel guilty.

> **"The planet is dying.**
> **_Our_ climate is warming up.**
> **_Our_ oceans are rising,**
> **_Our_ air is polluted.**
> **Species are becoming extinct."**

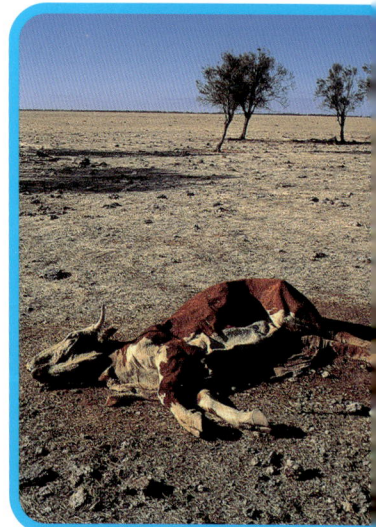

The writer uses sharp, short phrases, all in the present tense. The writer is stating facts for the reader. Also note the use of the pronoun "our" instead of the word "the". The writer is implying that these problems belong to all of us. It is everyone's responsibility.

> **" Join an environmental group today. Good intentions are not good enough! _Act now._ Before it is too late!"**

The writer presents a solution. It is in the form of a command so it is much stronger. And the writer is assuming that the reader has good intentions, but this is not enough. Another short command is used to indicate that failure to do so could result in disaster. Exclamation marks are also used to give a sense of urgency and emphasis.

> **" Our oceans' biggest _KILLER_ is not the shark."**

On page 11, the reader is hit by a very powerful statement. The writer is also using a well-known "fact" that the shark is seen by many as a killer. Note how the word "killer" is emphasised and enlarged so it stands out. The word is also a very strong one and has a powerful impact. The writer then surprises the reader by presenting something that is far more dangerous at work in the ocean.

Then we see an image of hundreds of plastic bags, and words are hardly necessary. Who would have thought an ordinary plastic bag would be a greater killer than a shark?

The flashing star behind these key words points directly to the image of the plastic bags. This immediately gets the reader's attention to the human creation which is causing problems in our oceans.

The reader is left to ponder the dangers that humans have created on the planet. The implication is that immediate action needs to be taken—avoid using plastic bags!

The Big Box of Nothing
—Now, in a New Larger Size

The environmentally sound product that every home can do without.

Endorsed by celebrities all over the world.

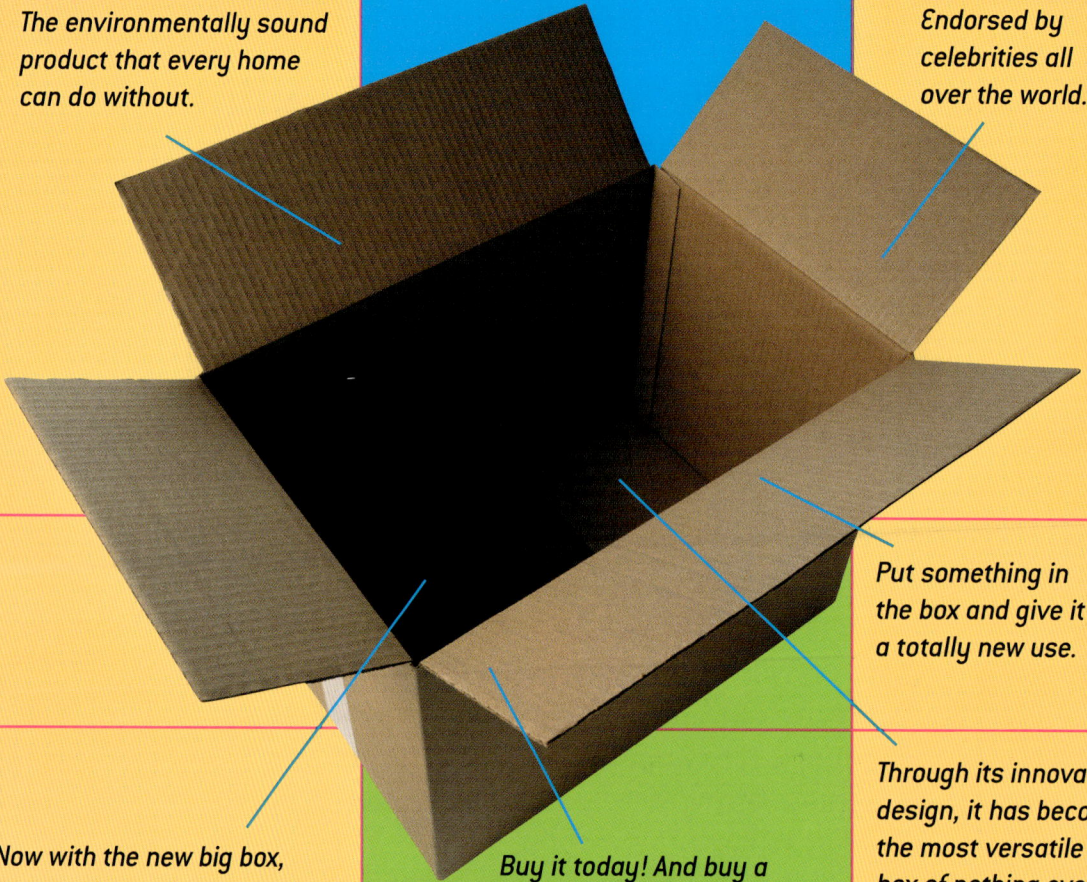

Put something in the box and give it a totally new use.

Now with the new big box, you can buy twice as much of nothing as you did before.

Buy it today! And buy a whole lot of expensive packaging that you can throw away tomorrow.

Through its innovative design, it has become the most versatile box of nothing ever produced—experience the difference.

Exploring Persuasive Texts— The Big Box of Nothing

We all buy items that we believe are right for us or meet our needs. To gain our attention, we are continually bombarded with eye-catching advertisements to persuade us to buy a product.

In the advertisement for **"The Big Box of Nothing"**, notice what is in the advertisement and what is not. For example, the price is missing. There is simply a picture of the Big Box of Nothing showing all its benefits. The advertisement is designed to create a mood. It wants people to feel something. It is not about price; its focus is image.

> **"…it has become the most versatile box of nothing ever produced—experience the _difference_."**

This statement implies that you must have this product as it can be used in any situation. You should be surprised that you have lived without this box for so long!

> **"Endorsed by _celebrities_ all over the world."**

Endorsement it a very important part of persuading the consumer. Rather than just taking the advertiser's word, you can trust and listen to celebrities from all over the world.

> **"The _environmentally sound_ product…"**

The advertisement is using emotive language here to play upon your conscience and to convince you that this really is the greatest Big Box of Nothing on the market.

It is very important for advertisers to hit the mark when devising an advertisement as they are very expensive to create. Would you buy the Big Box of Nothing?

Girl Seriously Injured by Rogue Bull Elephant

By our Sri Lankan reporter

IN THE EARLY HOURS of Friday morning, in a remote village in central Sri Lanka, a three-year-old girl was seriously injured by a wild bull elephant. Shyanthri Chandana was asleep in the family hut when the attack occurred.

The girl is in hospital in a serious condition with extensive bruising and fractures to the legs but she is lucky to be alive. The girl's brothers and sisters were bruised and shaken, though miraculously, they all escaped serious injury.

According to an eye-witness, the animal was trumpeting wildly. The elephant seemed to be panicked and confused as it crashed into the small hut where the girl was sleeping with her brothers and sisters. There is no evidence to suggest that the elephant targeted the girl. Tragically, it would appear that she was simply too close to the stampeding elephant.

Elephants, such as this one, sometimes rampage through villages.

As family members managed to scramble from the collapsed hut, they helped Shyanthri's father search through the wreckage of the hut until he found her. The girl's parents carried her two kilometres to the nearest available medical assistance.

Other villagers feared for the safety of their families and property as the elephant rampaged its way through the village. Despite the efforts of the village men, it took quite some time to chase the elephant away. Fortunately, no other villagers were harmed.

Blood was found along the path the elephant took to enter the village. Village leaders think it is likely the animal had been injured before the tragedy occurred.

Leaders of the local villages have banded together to demand that the government acts. They are insisting that measures be introduced to protect the people and their property from the almost constant threat from elephants. Several people have been seriously injured by rogue elephants and at least twenty families have had their crops damaged by the animals this year alone.

Animal experts are pushing for all elephants to be moved to national parks. Sri Lanka does not currently have enough national parks to accommodate its elephant population, but there are plans to expand the area available to create new national parks and join up the existing parks.

Village elders want to know when the government is going to take their concerns seriously.

Elephants and villagers working in harmony. Unfortunately, this is not always the case.

Readers Have Their Say

Here is a reader's response to the newspaper article, "Girl Seriously Injured by Rogue Bull Elephant".

Dear Editor,

I was appalled by the article "Girl Seriously Injured by Rogue Bull Elephant" in which you suggested creating more national parks in Sri Lanka. I say no to more national parks. I say people before elephants.

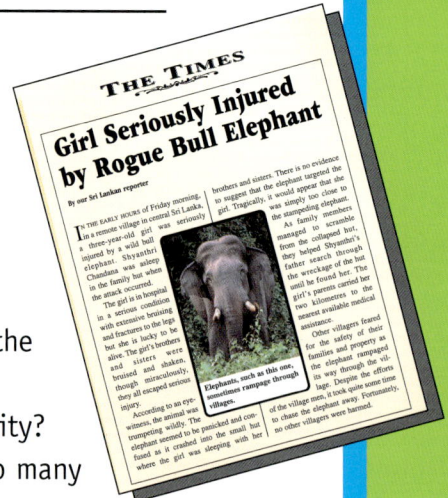

What about the villages that are already on the land that you want to give to the national park system? Where would those people go—to the city? The cities are overcrowded. There are already too many people living in poverty in the slums.

I say no more national parks for elephants. Surely we must put the welfare of the people first. After the floods of recent years, stocks of grain are dangerously low. The country needs all its farming land to feed its people. National parks are a luxury that Sri Lanka cannot afford.

Survival for people in Sri Lanka is already difficult enough. The only solution to the elephant problem is to control the population. Selective culling of adult elephants will reduce the numbers to a manageable amount. This will minimise the risk of attacks. Fewer elephants will require less land and this will allow a better balance of land use. People are more important than animals, and therefore have a moral right to use their country for their own needs before those of other creatures.

It's time to take a stand against animal rights and put people first!

Chandra Sala

Editor's Comment

Dear Chandra Sala,

Life is definitely tough for many villagers in Sri Lanka. There is no question that the Sri Lankan people need to have their homes and livelihood protected. But organised killing is not the answer. There are ways of preserving the habitats of native elephants without making things worse for the people. The most balanced use of the land would be to enable the people and the animals to live in harmony.

I suspect that the stampeding elephant had been injured by a trap set to keep the animals away from the village. It is most important for the villagers to think of effective, humane methods of preventing elephants from entering their villages.

Sri Lanka will never have enough farming land to support its population. Modern farming methods that will increase the yield of the land must be introduced. Increased productivity would enable the allocation of more land to national parks. Until these measures can be introduced, reasonable compensation should be paid promptly to families whose crops are damaged.

Sri Lanka, along with the rest of the world, has a moral obligation to preserve the environmental balance. People live in an environment that includes plants and animals. If the animals disappear, we alter the environment which, in turn, may no longer be able to support human life. We must work together to save the animals and forests or we might become an endangered species ourselves!

Signed **Ed.**

Exploring
Persuasive Texts
—Girl Seriously Injured by Rogue Bull Elephant

The newspaper article on pages 16 and 17 reports on an incident in which a three-year-old girl was seriously injured by an elephant that rampaged through a Sri Lankan village. The article is objective in its reporting of the incident and presents the views of the village leaders and the animal experts in a fair and impartial manner.

The letter on page 18, "Readers Have Their Say", is a reader's response to the article. The writer writes from the viewpoint that humans are more important than animals. She uses strong, emotive language to convince the reader to take a stand against animal rights.

> "I say *no* to more national parks. I say people before elephants."

Here, the first person tense is used and the language is strong and outraged. The phrase, "I say no" is repeated again further on in the letter for additional impact.

> "After the floods of recent years, stocks of grain are *dangerously* low."

The writer emphasises her viewpoint by including a fact. Note how a fact is stated without the addition of statistics to support her assertion of low grain stocks. A descriptive adverb (the word "dangerously") is used, too.

> "The *only solution* to the elephant problem is to control the population."

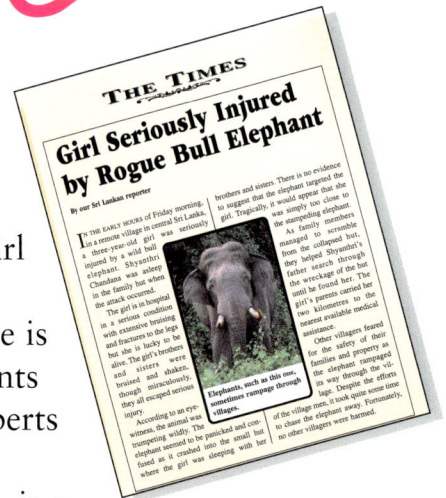

The writer doesn't present any other alternative. The writer also omits any reference to the endangerment of elephants.

In "Editor's Comment" on page 19, the editor appears to be striking a balance between two viewpoints and purposely uses the words "balanced" and "harmony". These words are intended to immediately make the reader believe that alternatives to culling elephants are possible.

> **"Life is definitely tough for many villagers in Sri Lanka. *There is no question* that the Sri Lankan people need to have their homes and livelihood protected."**

The editor begins by addressing the concerns raised in the letter and states that this is a fact that should not be questioned.

> **"I *suspect* that the stampeding elephant had been injured by a trap set to keep the animals away from the village."**

By using the words "I suspect", the editor is making it clear that he or she is not completely sure of the accuracy of the fact and it is very much a personal opinion of Chandra Sala. The editor is also implying that those people who were attempting to trap the elephants must take some blame for the incident. The editor is proving that trapping is not an effective solution to the problem.

> **"Sri Lanka, along with the rest of the world, has a *moral* obligation to preserve the environmental balance."**

Note the use of the word "moral". The editor concludes by stating that this issue goes beyond the concern of Sri Lanka; it is a world problem. He or she appeals to the reader by giving a depressing scenario of the future if the viewpoint expressed in the letter is followed.

Introduction to Discussion Texts

The aim of a discussion text is to present both sides of an issue. The information must be balanced so that the reader can weigh up the positive and negative aspects being presented without the pressure of bias. It is really like a debate in writing.

The text usually begins with the arguments "for" the issue under discussion, followed by the arguments "against" the issue. A recommendation will then follow. This recommendation is purely the writer's opinion based on the information presented, not one that is necessarily adopted by the reader. Once you have read an entire discussion text, you should be equipped with enough information to formulate your own conclusion and develop your own responses and ideas.

On pages 24–29, you will find an argument for and an argument against a controversial issue—packaging.

Not everyone agrees on this issue, and there are no easy answers. After you have read about the issue, you may wish to discuss what you have read. Before beginning a discussion, consider the following points.

1 When putting forward a point of view, you are aiming to persuade your listeners to accept it and perhaps adopt it themselves. Before beginning to speak, be sure of what you want to say and how you want to say it.

2 Be prepared for counter-arguments. Think about how your points of view may be argued against, and have answers ready.

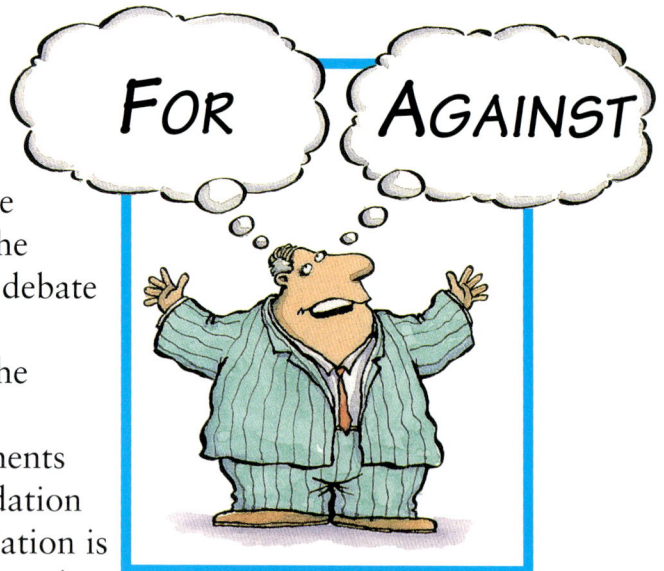

3 If possible, support your case with statistics, photographs, quotes from experts, and so on.

4 Be prepared to listen to opposing views, and think about them carefully.

5 After the discussion, take time to think about how well you put across your point of view. Are there lessons to be learned for future discussions?

Forms of Discussion Texts:
Newspaper articles, essays, documentaries, debates

Purpose:
To examine issues from two or more points of view and make a final recommendation or assessment.

Structure:
- State the issue in a straightforward, clear manner supported by background information.
- State an argument for the issue with supportive evidence.
- Use evaluative language, for example, "causing".
- State an argument against the issue with supportive evidence.
- Use phrases that introduce an opposing point of view, for example, "on the other hand".
- Use conjunctions that introduce an opposing point of view, for example, "although", "however".
- Use figures and percentages to clarify information.
- Discussions end with a conclusion and a recommendation or assessment. This may mean discussing points raised in both the for and against discussions, and trying to strike a balance or reach a middle point.

Packaging—More Is Best

**Percy Parcel, from the Packaging Association
presents his point of view on packaging.**

From the packager's point of view, how much is enough when it comes to wrapping things up? Packaging is essential.

It is necessary for the protection of goods. Consumers want to be confident that whatever they buy, whether it be a packet of chocolate biscuits or a new DVD TV, that the goods in the shop have been packaged properly so that they will not be damaged or broken when they get them home.

Packaging is also necessary to protect customers against illness. Food must be packaged so that it will not go off and so that it cannot be tampered with.

I've been in the packaging business for many years and I know what consumers want. They want attractive packaging—colourful, high quality and distinctive. Customers want to be able to easily recognise their favourite brands among a sea of items for sale. In response to this, we packagers are constantly developing new and innovative ways to package products.

Developments in packaging cost money. This has to be added to the price of the goods. This is only fair because it is the customer who demands a certain standard of packaging. We know from experience that people want to buy goods with eye-catching and secure packaging.

There's also the producer's and retailer's needs to consider. They want lightweight protective packaging because the less a product weighs, the less it costs to transport. Lightweight packaging is expensive to develop and introduce. But it is cost-effective in the long run because it is cheaper to transport and it minimises damage, which reduces the number of items being returned and replaced.

It's all very well to go on about minimal packaging and preserving resources. But I say, if a job's worth doing, it's worth doing well. Why take risks by cutting the amount of packaging to the bare bones. We have to give the customers what they want. And for the few who don't want it? Well, we're certainly not forcing anyone to buy something they don't want. And that's a fact!

Packaging is one of the fruits of modern technology. There will always be someone who wants to go back to the way things were, but they're a minority. The proof is in the buying—people are buying goods the way we package them! Obviously, we are providing what the customer wants—sturdy, safe, high quality, attractive packaging. We must be realistic about our packaging needs and not give in to the green fringe.

Packaging
—Take Care or Buyer Beware!

Our environmentally-aware writer, Jennifer Green, responds to Percy Parcel's point of view.

The Earth is groaning under the weight of packaging. You and I can no longer afford to ignore the cost— the waste of money and the environmental damage are crippling.

When I see people buying toys as gifts, for example, they are already packaged in plastic and cardboard, and then either wrapped in paper or put into a bag.

A lot of non-renewable resources are used up just to package one doll or action figure. Trees must be chopped down in order to make paper and cardboard. This is a perfect example of excessive and unnecessary packaging that wastes our money and our natural resources. Not to mention the damage done to the atmosphere from the fumes and gases released into the air during the manufacturing process.

Packaging must be made only from environmentally-friendly materials and should be used only when absolutely necessary. I think that, as consumers, it is time that we took the responsibility for packaging into our own hands. For most of the items we purchase, we could provide our own packaging to transport it in. Shopping carts, baskets or fabric shopping bags are adequate for most of the products we purchase. Large items, such as refrigerators and washing machines could be packaged in re-useable cloth covers. Manufacturers could charge a deposit on these covers to ensure that the customers returned them.

Most packaging creates waste which must then be disposed of. Non-biodegradable products such as plastics must be stored in the earth itself. Sooner or later, we'll run out of areas to use for land-fill—then what? Already, too many waste products end up in our waterways and oceans. Marine plants and animals are killed by plastic bags and ties that tangle and suffocate them.

Start a responsible packaging program in your own home, today. There's no need to wrap up everything for your school lunch and then put it into a bag that you'll throw away. Instead, you can use a lunchbox, and bring it home to be used again and again.

I say don't burden our Earth any longer! Change your habits now. Minimal, environmentally-friendly packaging is achievable and it's our responsibility—yours and mine.

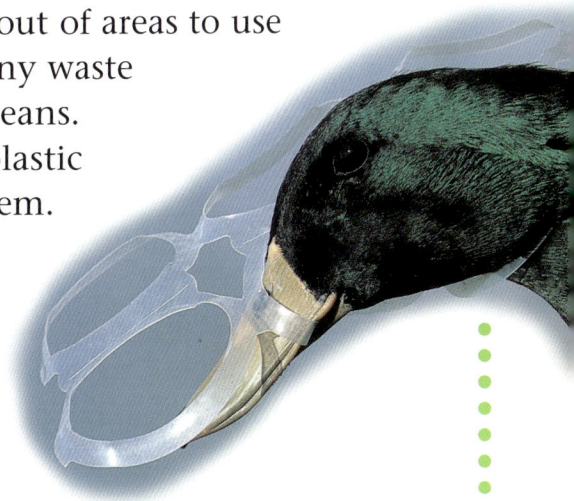

What's the Answer?

Let's hear what a local shopkeeper has to say and how he sees both sides of the argument.

Daniel, the local shopkeeper, sees the arguments for and against packaging.

In the arguments for and against packaging, it's easy to see that both sides have some valid points to make. Yet, as with all discussions, there is a middle ground.

Some things definitely need to be packaged. Protection from damage and loss of freshness is important. In this day and age, customers expect to get value for their money. They will not buy products that are broken or spoiled. So I cannot afford to receive products for sale that are damaged or stale. It costs me time and money to return and replace products that are unsaleable.

As a shopkeeper, I must supply what my customers want. But in order to have customers, I must attract people into my shop. Packaging is one of the ways that I do this. Colourful and distinctive packaging can be used to create attractive displays that please the customers when they enter my shop. Customers can tell easily what brands I have available. They can also tell from the information on the packaging whether the goods suit their needs.

On the other hand, there are ways of minimising the impact of packaging by using as little as possible and making sure that what is used is recyclable or biodegradable.

Some things have a natural package, such as the skin of an avocado or a banana that is airtight and waterproof. These foods do not need any other packaging.

Some people bring their own bags and baskets to the shop and buy as many things as they can without packaging. They still take everything home in a bag, but there is much less packaging to dispose of and the bags can be used again on their next shopping trip.

Packaging does not need to be extravagant and expensive. It only needs to be functional. The job of protecting the goods that we buy and sell can be done with as little packaging as possible and in a simple form. Packaging that is clean, clear and practical will serve the dual purpose of protecting the goods and the environment. And that's the middle ground. Manufacturers need to provide the necessary packaging but not use resources to create excessive packaging.

We can make choices every day about the amount of packaging we consume by being choosy about the things we buy.

Some customers prefer to use their own bags and baskets to cut down on the amount of packaging.

Exploring
Discussion Texts
—Packaging

In "PACKAGING—More Is Best" on pages 24 and 25, the writer presents his viewpoint for packaging.

> ❝Consumers want to be **confident** that whatever they buy … will not be damaged or broken when they get them home.❞

> ❝Packaging is also **necessary** to protect customers against illness.❞

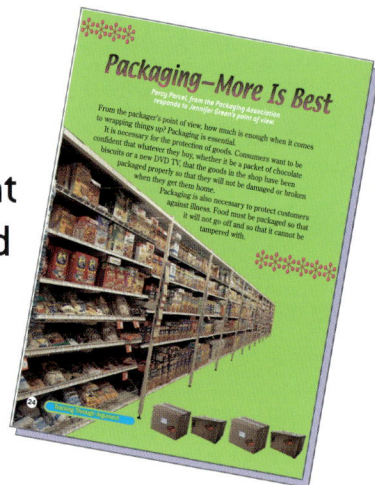

The writer begins by involving the reader as the consumer, although the first person tense is not used. The writer assumes that consumers want undamaged goods and hygienic packaging.

> ❝I've been in the packaging business for many years and I **know** what consumers want.❞

The writer is using his personal knowledge to convince the reader. He is the expert. Note the use of the first person.

> ❝There's also the **producer's** and **retailer's** needs to consider.❞

It is also clear that the writer, Percy Parcel from the Packaging Association, is representing the views of the producers and retailers.

> ❝Packaging is one of the fruits of **modern technology**. There will always be someone who wants to go back to the way things were, but they're a **minority**.❞

The writer is reminding the reader that we live in the modern world with modern technology and people should look forward, not backwards. He also states that those with opposing views are in the minority and he has stated this as a fact although no evidence is produced to support this statement.

In "PACKAGING—Take Care or Buyer Beware!" on pages 26 and 27, the reader is presented with an emotive appeal against packaging in both the text and the images used.

> **"You and I** can no longer afford to ignore the cost—the **waste** of money and the environmental **damage** are **crippling**.**"**

The writer is quick to bring the reader into the situation so the reader begins to question the need for packaging. The writer avoids alienating the reader by including herself in the sentence. Emotive words are used.

> **"**Packaging **must** be made only from environmentally-friendly materials and **should** be used only when absolutely necessary.**"**

Note the use of the words "must" and "should"; a strong imperative use of language.

> **"**Marine plants and animals are **killed** by plastic bags and ties that tangle and **suffocate** them.**"**

Emotive images and words are used here, such as "killed" and "suffocate". The writer does acknowledge that some packaging is necessary and she suggests more environmentally-friendly packaging options. But the writer states that a change in attitude must be adopted and points out that it is everyone's responsibility.

The writer's style is chatty and informal so the personal tone will sway the reader. The writer also uses exclamation marks to emphasise important points.

In "What's the Answer?" on pages 28 and 29, a balanced view is presented in order to develop the discussion.

> ❝Some things definitely **need** to be packaged. Protection from damage and loss of freshness is important.❞

The writer is stating the view that some things require packaging and this was acknowledged in both the for and against discussions.

> ❝On the other hand, there are ways of **minimising the impact** of packaging by using as little as possible and **making sure** that what is used is recyclable or biodegradable.❞

> ❝Packaging does not need to be extravagant and expensive. It only needs to be **functional**.❞

The writer is now presenting his viewpoint which is the middle ground and putting forward a solution. Less packaging and more environmentally-friendly packaging is best. Functionality should be the main focus of packaging. The writer's style is less emotive than the previous two articles and no exclamation marks are used. The writer is supporting his viewpoint from his experience as a shopkeeper.

The writer concludes by stating that each of us needs to choose carefully when buying goods. It is at this stage that the reader can use all the information presented to form his or her own opinion about the packaging issue.